ESTRANGED
& other American poems, 2019-2022

ELIZABETH ELLEN

for all those from whom I am estranged...

but, most especially, for N and N

better to wait til after the disappointment seeps in,
honey: my(unsolicited)(writing) advice to you.

February, 2019

#1

I hadn't written a poem or taken a photograph of
myself in three years
This was how I knew I was in love
I wanted something tangible to give him

The best thing about him was he liked my poems
That wasn't the best thing but it was one thing.
The best thing about him, I knew, I hadn't discovered
yet
It was waiting for me – this thing – somewhere in the
future.
I saw my future self discovering it: this best thing
about him.
I stared at my future self with envy
It was hard being patient
I remembered that a dead writer had said something
about anticipation
Being the purest form of pleasure
But my future self knew that was bullshit (my present
self knew it, too – this was what we had in common)
My future self, the one I envied, knew the purest form
of pleasure was discovering
This best thing about him.
My future self was a bitch like that.
I hated my future self but there was something like
hope in her existence.

#2

Sometimes I talked to the man's photograph
The one at the back of the book or the one he'd sent
me
Either one, it didn't matter
Sometimes I said, "I wish you were old and ugly then
maybe this would all be okay"
Even though I knew it wouldn't matter.
Women didn't care about small things like a man's
looks
When a man had written a book and the book was on
the front table of a bookstore
Especially when the man had had an addiction to
a glamorous drug or a drug women in bookstores
considered glamorous
Still, I wanted the man to be old and ugly and mine
He couldn't get old or ugly fast enough (for me)
I'd already written him a forty thousand word letter
I was never going to send
Unless he got really old and really ugly, fast
Then maybe I would consider telling him everything.
Until that happened, though, I would keep my secrets
to myself.
(Every secret started with the word "dear" followed
by the man's name)
(There were a lot of dears, a lot of secrets)
I didn't know how to tell him everything as long as he
looked the way he looked
The man said, "I'm not pretty like you" but I knew
he was lying.

#3

when the man and I had first started talking
we'd agreed on something: *love is hell*
that was what we said, what we agreed on
I think I knew then, as we were agreeing on love being
hell
That I was going to fall in love with him
That's the kind of conversation you only have with
someone
You know you're going to fall in love with
"Love is hell. Haha," you say, you agree, like it's a light
joke,
like you aren't soon going to be driving thirty extra
miles home from Target
listening to bad metal bands because only bad metal
bands get you now,
only bad metal bands know your pain.

#4

the man had written a book and I had written a book and we each read each other's books in lieu of normal dating

because circumstances on both ends prevented normal dating.

instead of going on dates and listening to each other tell stories

we read each other's books and the stories contained within them

the stories were similar and different from the stories we would have

told had we been on real dates at IHOP or Denny's or wherever

At IHOP or Denny's we would have been provided the opportunity

To ask follow up questions, and to lie or to tell the truth

Which was sort of like writing a book except the person would be sitting across from you

Making it harder (and easier) to do both

The strangest part about reading the man's book in lieu of dating was

Constantly being aware of the man's ex

THERE SHE WAS ON PRACTICALLY EVERY PAGE

And here I was on no page

Of course her presence (on the page) only made me want the man more

Every time the man (in the book) called her (the fictional ex) on the telephone

I pinched the flesh on the inside of my thigh real hard

Sometimes I stopped reading to wonder what the man did

When reading about my ex

If he pinched his leg or winced or something else

It made me smile a little to think of the man wincing

By the end of the book the insides of my thighs were red and a little puffy

From all that pinching.

It wasn't like sex but it wasn't not like fucking, either.

#5

I was in my basement watching a David Foster
Wallace movie on my laptop
And drinking herbal tea spiked with rum
The night before I had drank too much Grand
Marnier and smoked too many cigarettes
And listened to U2 who I don't even really like
Due to feelings of inadequacy and frustration and
longing
I had fucked up a phone call or a series of phone calls
due to my not having
A smart phone and due to my being dumb and scared
And now I was experiencing feelings of self-loathing
and regret because of it

A week before my friend had told me to watch the
David Foster Wallace movie
She'd said she'd watched it five times already and that
it made her feel relaxed
Just to have it on, playing in the background of
whatever else she was doing.
I wasn't doing anything else, though, just drinking my
spiked tea and smoking
My cigarettes

I didn't know how I felt about David Foster Wallace
Or I didn't know how I felt about the man portraying
David foster Wallace on my laptop
I thought about the man I was in love with and
someone portraying him on a screen
I didn't know how I would feel about that, either
Part of me wanted to listen to U2 again even though
I didn't really even like U2
part of me wanted to finish reading infinite jest
mostly I just felt jealous of the man following David
Foster Wallace around on his book tour
I wanted to follow the man I was in love with around,
similarly; ask him questions
Stand to the side while he read in front of a crowd; sit
on a motel bed opposite him after the reading, eating
candy bars and laughing.
Maybe listen to U2.

#6

My husband and I had sex once every four to six
weeks when I made a reservation at a hotel
If I didn't make a reservation we didn't have sex
(if I didn't do anything we didn't have sex)
I couldn't stop thinking about my friend and her
husband having sex three times a week
I got online and made a search of apartment
complexes in my area
I remembered when I'd gotten divorced the first time
How it'd been the happiest year of my life
Dancing around my shitty apartment living room
every night with a cigarette
And a beer while my daughter slept
Now my daughter was a grown up, moving into an
apartment with her boyfriend
There were other reasons I was searching apartment
complexes in my area
Reasons having to do with finances and money owed
a bank and feelings of loneliness
If I was going to spend 85% of my time alone in a
bedroom I might as well
Spend 100% of my time alone in an apartment
I thought one day I might want to be with someone
who wanted to have sex with me
- three times a week, more on weekends – someone
who might want to hold my face in his hands
I didn't want to have to make any more hotel
reservations
(no one held my face in his hands)
I printed out the info for four apartment complexes
in town
I thought about the type of beer I would buy when I
moved into one.
Molson or Heineken. Something in a green bottle.
I thought about drinking one, sitting cross legged on
my shitty new tan carpet,
Blowing cigarette smoke out the patio door, because
no one lets you smoke in apartment complexes
anymore.

#7

"a person can live on so little," a man I admired had said. "a person can live on almost nothing."
I knew the man I admired was right.
The night before I'd had a dream about the man. my husband was in the dream, too.
My husband was in a kitchen, cooking, and the man and I were lying together on a bed.
"We can't have sex yet," I said to the man and the man had said "I know" and we had
lay on the bed together, my face pressed into his t-shirt, and it had felt good, as good as sex, but maybe I was forgetting.

the last time I had had a dream about the man my husband had been in the dream also
we'd been at a party, in the dream, and talking to the man
my husband had said, "Come on, let's go" and I had hesitated
I hadn't wanted to go; I had wanted to stay with the man
Finally, the man had said, "she wants to stay" or "I want her to stay," I forget which
My husband had shrugged his shoulders
My husband never fought anything or fought for anything (including/especially me)
Then the man and I were in a back room and the man leaned down to kiss me
It wasn't one of those sloppy kinds of kisses with a lot of tongue, which are nice too
It was one of those old-fashioned movie kisses where your lips are pressed together but closed and you just stay like that for what feels like an eternity
And when I woke in the morning I touched my lips with my finger
I kept touching my lips all day
Sometimes I closed my eyes to try to remember better
My husband never noticed

I kept touching my lips.
I knew I could live on so little.

#8

She had one goal in life (now)
(Which was) to have sex with the man before she died
She didn't believe in fate anymore -
She had decided; she had decided this one night
while drinking a large amount of champagne left her
by her mother.
(she tried not to think of what Hemingway had said
about Zelda's health
and her drinking large quantities of champagne while
she drank the champagne)
(The man liked A Moveable Feast, also; it was a
common thread of conversation
between the two of them.)
She didn't believe in love, either
She believed in having sex with a man she admired
She hoped he would light a cigarette for each of them,
after -
This man she admired. (This man who admired
Hemingway.)
This was her only remaining goal in life
This and to marry the man, also
But first she would have to attain a divorce.
(But first she would have to reduce the amount of
champagne she was now,
nightly, drinking.)

BIRTHDAY POEM

I wasn't going to write you this poem
        I was reading *the bell jar* & then I was
reading *ariel* ...
        can you imagine being ted hughes?

I bet *you* can!

I would never end up raving mad

despite what I said
        I have too much pride/narcissistic interest
in myself/my work

but also: I thought we were *friends*
        (read: I thought it didn't matter
        who either of us sleeps with)

        (maybe we should have told ppl
        I was your sister, like in a 1930s
        Screwball comedy, so no one
        Could be jealous of me or question
        My presence in your life)
        (but also so you wouldn't scare off any men
I might meet
        while standing next to you)

I think I would make a real good sister, actually

I think sylvia plath wrote a poem
        Called birthday present
        in *ariel* ("I do no want much of a present,
anyway, this year.
        after all I am alive only by accident." So
dramatic!)

I think ted hughes wrote a collection of poems
        Called *birthday letters*
        For sylvia

19 years after she died
a couple months before he did

he must have been a pretty good lay
            ted hughes, I mean
            idk, some men are just like that
                so good at fucking you'll put up w almost
anything
you'll stick your head in an oven, even, if they stop
giving it to you (the dick) and give it to someone else
instead (the dick) (and then stop giving it to her and
giving it to someone else and so and and so on like a
shampoo commercial I remember from the 80s)!

Confession: today I finally shaved my head

It was fucking dismal!

I don't want to think further than *that*!

Few things have ever felt as good
            (don't worry: I won't be celibate!)

It just suddenly occurred to me (now that this poem
is almost over)
            That for this to be a 'good poem'
            (read: *academic*)
            I would need to add some references
            To Greek mythology
            Or to Shakespeare, maybe Beowulf,
            Maybe Homer? IDK ...

(referencing s. plath doesn't count!) (no one has ever
confused me for an academic!)

QUARANTINE

Day 23 or 24, who can remember
I went to bed early the night before only to find I
couldn't sleep
I lay in bed considering the option I didn't feel
anything anymore
"Is this boredom, or something else?" I spoke aloud
to the ceiling fan
I didn't have an answer.
Eventually I got out of bed,
Ate some raspberries, read a page or two of Andy
Warhol's *Diaries*

Someone had pulled off Andy's wig at a book signing
He could barely speak about it
Still, the next day he went *here* and *here* and *there*,
Saw *this* person and *that* person and *this* person
What luxury! I thought (his maneuverings about the
city so effortlessly)
It all felt so far away, now – a life of socializing
A life in which you can be publicly humiliated
In front of your friends (the kidnapping of a wig!)

I got back in bed
I was still with the feeling of boredom
But now, at least, I could sleep
Or I thought I might ...
            It was increasingly hard to decipher

DAY 23 OR 24

... and who knows what these numbers refer to
Am I speaking of the virus or something else?
I don't want to think about *it*, in either case

I will, instead, read Sartre, Rilke, Valery ...
Anyone writing in the past of ennui that feels, now,
Almost comical
What did they have to feel nauseous about?
They had their cafés, their liquors, their debates, their
women!

The worst thing to happen to any of them:
Waking up an insect!
That has a certain luxurious feel to it, now, also
            Like Warhol's menagerie of wigs!
            (all those synchronized utilitarian legs!)

I woke this morning wondering if rather than
boredom
It was a sort of numbness
A subconscious stilling of emotion

Whatever it was I felt somnambulistic
As in the past (life)

I padded into the kitchen to make coffee with eyes
shut or open
I wasn't sure (it didn't matter; I knew the route)
I was thinking of Jean-Michael (Basquiat)
My obsession with finding his name in Warhol's
diaries
(I highlighted it yellow in every entry, as though
illuminating his face for some secret pleasure)
My obsession with reading about his ever-changing
roster of women
It was 1985 (in the diary); he would be dead in three
years
He was living as though he knew it

I thought:
Good for Jean-Michael! (I applauded each new woman
gallery opening, the extravagance of overpriced hotel
rooms, the five minute tying of a shoe ...)

Maybe it was quarantining –
That had me feeling this way:
        Bored, numb, unnauseous ...

I so often confused the causes
Of my maladies (or lack thereof)

To make this poem really come together
I should make some sort of analogy between
Quarantining from the virus
And quarantining from you

(or would that be a metaphor?)

Protecting myself in either/both cases

(I am always so dumb when it comes to technical
terms such as analogy and metaphor)

But doing so – making that analogy –
        Even merely thinking of doing so
Bores me to tears!

(I don't really care: the difference)

It would be so easy
        Even a preschool child could see the
comparison

Am I preventing a spread? I would ask myself
In this poem, were it to be another clichéd analogy

Am I the infected or the infector?
I would ponder, so sillily,
Ever the precocious toddler (or thinking myself so)

Rather than a grown woman
Who has no need to ponder such questions (the questions I knew to be irrelevant)

I thought of texting you a photograph from the protest Wednesday
I thought of calling you to tell you everything I was seeing ...

But something in me – the boredom or numbness or something else unnamed I have yet to pinpoint –

Kept me from doing so

i left my phone, instead, in the glove box

maybe I didn't want to interrupt you
maybe now I always feel I will be an interruption (something I am loathe to feel)

I wonder if this is boredom or numbness or something else ... somnambulism?
As I plunge my coffee
And then, finally, I feel my eyes wetting
And I think, "Good. They are open."

BIRTHDAY PRESENT [4.19.20]

for -

This wasn't supposed to be a poem

I said, *"Fuck this shit."*

No one heard me. We were all, by now, twenty-two
days into self-quarantine.

I went down into my basement;
        Lit a cigarette.

It burned burned burned
        Just like the Johnny Cash song (said it
would)
The cigarette, of course, but also this thing inside me
        This thing...
Whatever you want to call it.
        this ...

(Once you said to me, "you're really murdering this"

"what is this?" I said

"this is this," you said

you were are such an asshole like that

this was is my least favorite/favorite thing about you

how much of an asshole you can be [smile]

I could can be an asshole too [wink]

This is my favorite thing about us:
        What assholes we are/can be.)

DAY 22

I was reading another Bukowski poem this morning
            In between taking turns at my coffee and
writing (you) another (this) poem

Bukowski was going on about a Mozart symphony
Mozart had
allegedly written
in one day

Bukowski said it had "enough wild and crazy joy to
last forever,
            Whatever forever is."

I thought about that
            "whatever forever is"
I thought:
            AS LONG AS YOU DON'T EVER
TELL ME YOU LOVE ME
            THIS WILL ALL BE OK.

POWER MOVES

I was okay til Tuesday
I wasn't smoking or drinking (while you were gone)
I was working on my writing
I was finishing another cynical story –
Maybe this was why you thought I'd be more cynical.

I was working on my cynical story
When suddenly I burst out sobbing.
Maybe this was why you'd thought I'd be more
cynical.

I knew if we were able to talk you'd tell me to have a
drink,
To go buy a pack of cigarettes. ("Power moves")

"It's important we're always friends," you or I said/ I
think you said.

I can't remember now.

It's been years now since I've talked to you.

(I wrote these last two lines in 2022. Power moves!)

#3

I could marry you for your shoeshining capabilities

I finally threw out the shoeshine kit you bought that day
At Walgreens

I remember the crappy tshirt hanging on a crappy hanger in the store I briefly considered buying as we passed by it looking for the shoeshine kit

Another regret!

No Walgreens I <3 Mississippi tshirt to wear while writing these poems

While watching another 30 for 30 on the stoop outside my Ohio rental

I threw out the shoeshine kit finally before my last move

The only line remaining from this original poem is the first one

I had forgotten all about the shoeshine kit, to tell you the truth

I'm starting to forget a lot abt that time (w you)

I can't tell if that's a good thing or a bad thing

I just wish I had that I <3 Mississippi shirt on while typing this poem.

#6 I wanted to burn this house down

did I ever tell you, when I got your letter –
toward the end of summer
the end of August

August 17th   *2019*

it was almost midnight, I remember
when I slipped on my flip flops
and stumbled – drunkenly– out to the mailbox
(even then I needed the protectiveness/the
numbingness of alcohol to handle my feelings for
you)
I had waited five whole days to check the mail
To increase the likelihood of a letter
Because checking the box every day was too painful
an activity (to engage in daily)
And anyway, there was your letter, telling me I
wouldn't be able to visit you, after all ... (Mr. Nicely
had nixed my visitation!)

I don't think I ever told you but I remember telling
myself – in my drunkenness, in my inebriation – I
wanted to burn the house down (and me in/with it)
(that night)

That's how disappointed I was not to be meeting you
I don't think I ever told you, is all.
(I think I didn't want you to feel bad)
but I'm telling you now. (Not so you'll feel bad, but
so you'll know:)
I wanted to burn this house down.

#16

don't hold these poems against me
meaning: don't punish me for telling you everything
okay, not *everything*, but *some* things
there is always so much more
I want to tell you
        I want to *ask*
So much closer I can press my face against your
sweater
        The one you were wearing that *memorable*
Saturday afternoon
        The one my tears dried into

(I wish your face still smelled like my face!)

I hope you haven't washed that sweater yet
I hope my tears are still in there ... *somewhere*
Amongst the Chinese food and cigarettes and shoe
polish and pizza

Don't tell me if they're not (if you washed it)
I don't want to know.

LAST POEM

The pain in my head
   Matched the pain in my heart.
Good! I thought – just what you deserve,
A reminder you can't take back ugly words.
   A reminder you proved to him, finally:
   You're not a beautiful person,
   You're not kind and good,
   You can be shitty like everyone else.
He was being shitty, too, in a way
   Letting you feel so bad about yourself
   (about you & him)
   knowing you were just hurting
   (hurting because he couldn't love you
   the way you wanted to be loved)
it's okay (it's not your fault)
   (it's not anyone's fault)
I poured the rest of the whiskey down the sink
   Broke my cigarettes in half
I stared at a Bukowski poem
   Pinned over my desk
Bukowski said, "I'd tell them to have an unhappy love affair,
   Hemorrhoids, bad teeth..."
   (when asked his advice for teaching creative
writing)
But I had a happy love affair, I thought
I couldn't stop thinking of all the things that
   Had made me happy
   (during this love affair):
the letters and 15 minute phone calls
the letters & his voice when I picked up
 "We'll always know each other and have secrets
   just between us"
Now my head hurt, and my heart, too.
   Good! I thought –
   Pain is a reminder
   Of how deeply you loved.
   Pain is a reminder: you were lucky

To know him.
You don't have to stop feeling grateful
        You don't have to stop feeling at all
The pain is only a reminder:
        Of all the secrets still in your heart.
Let them be (the secrets!)
        It will be ok. You'll be ok. You were lucky
once.

Kid Rock Trucker Hat

I had slept one hour and then I hadn't slept for four
Something about not having eaten and thinking
about you
Something about a Johnny Cash biography I was
reading:
there were so many more
women
than Vivian and June (why do the movies always lie?)
I got out of bed and put on my Kid Rock trucker hat
I made a pair of waffles in the toaster and went
upstairs
I thought, *maybe now I can write something good for him*
(read: you)
again
now that I have on my Kid Rock trucker hat.

Cynical

I was sitting in my basement
I'd gotten good at cigarettes again
I could smoke eight at a time now
All in one sitting!

I could feel my lungs struggling when I walked the
dog at night
Sometimes I didn't smoke for a day – to give them
a rest

Other ways I was good with cigarettes now: burning
a hole in my arm
I did this to impress you - did you know that? are you
impressed?

I was watching the movie *Hoosiers* at the time
I wanted to be as good as a man
Or as bad
Burning a hole in my arm   while watching a movie
abt basketball

Not being cynical.
I'm not being cynical in this poem at all.

OHIO

I had had this plan for a while
It was a plan for when things ended

I had the sense one day I would be done
I had the sense everything would cause me too much
pain

I knew one day I wouldn't want to feel anything
anymore
I had the sense Ohio was the place to go to not feel
anything anymore
(I'd lived there before so I knew)

My plan was to move to someone's small obscure
hometown (not mine)
Change my phone number, get rid of my laptop,
forget about email
My plan was to stop talking to anyone who was or had
ever been a writer/publisher/editor
Or agent (yes, Scott and Julia, too)
My plan was to write you a letter (secretly), make you
promise not to disclose to anyone else my location
(no, not even Scott and Julia)

We had written letters before
We could write letters again

This, I had decided, was how we could always be
friends
There wasn't any other way

OHIO II

My plan was to drink Michelob Light at a bar where
persons from my high school went to drink
(the ones who weren't dead yet)
my plan was to smoke cigarettes that weren't Benson
& Hedges outside the bar
with people from my high school
(the ones who hadn't od'd or killed themselves yet)

my plan was to write but to not publish (like a 'true
artist' or loser or whatever)
to live in this small Ohio town
die in obscurity
die with shit on my computer that would or wouldn't
be published (it wouldn't matter)
die still being friends with you

I would be there in my kitchen, drinking Michelob
Light
Smoking Kool unfiltered
Not caring about anything as small as death
Your letters in a pile on the table
A candle lit so I could read them

A guy from my high school recently gone ...

If you wanted to come over
Have a drink and a smoke with me
Die the way people are meant to die (in Ohio) (with
me).

Long Distance

A friend we had in common kept saying, "that's who
you should go for"
Any time I mentioned any man who wasn't you

For the longest time I thought the friend we had in
common was full of shit
Or jealous

I kept on answering, "But it's too late. I like ----"
(and instead of the dashes were the letters of your
name)

then I started to think the friend we had in common
knew something I didn't know

I think the whole worlds knows
There was something I didn't know.

#10

[I don't like #10 anymore. But here is where #10 would go if #10 still existed, other than on a sheet of paper thrown in the trash. It doesn't matter. that's what the poem said. it said *blah blah blah blah blah*.]

February 4th, 2020

We didn't have a fight tonight
Because I wouldn't let us
everything was so precarious
Because of long distance
And because you were already dealing with so much;

Later I was reading a biography of Johnny Cash
And in the section I was reading Johnny and June got
in a big fight
And June stormed off to take a shower in her hotel
room and Johnny took her clothes back to his room
and locked the door so June couldn't get dressed and
leave him.

I didn't want to fight with you on account of us being
long distance
But part of me fantasized about fighting with you in
person – just once,

so we could finally make up

But it was too big a risk to take –
Long distance.

Also, everything seemed so silly written down in a
text message
Rather than screamed inside of a hotel room.
(I had typed out some texts and deleted them.)
(I wasn't taking a shower; you weren't in the other
room.)
(we couldn't make up now and that was the worst
part of this whole imagined scenario.)

Fortune Cookie Fortune

a few hours after we didn't have the fight I texted you
to remind you of the fortune cookie fortune

I was trying to get us back on track,
Away from the fight we weren't having/didn't have
I think it was in our minds, anyway,
The fight
We weren't having

So I said, "Don't forget our fortune cookie fortune"

I said the dinner we shared alone together was my
favorite part

But really it was my second favorite part

I didn't know yet you'd put the fortune cookie fortune
in my purse
I didn't know because I'd slid my phone under the
couch again like I always do
When I'm drunk and insecure,
Rather than wait to see if you text back.

I wouldn't know for twenty-four hours
Til I used the stick from the sliding glass door to dig
my phone out from under the couch

But then there it was – just like you said in your text!
– the fortune cookie fortune
at the bottom of my purse.

And I thought, hmmm, maybe he *does* love me.
And then I thought, it doesn't matter; those are just
words.

#19 another 'last poem'

that last poem is the most selfish poem I've ever written
I don't really mean it – about hoping the Coronavirus is real.
I was just looking for any excuse to forget my dignity.
I was just looking for any reason to talk to you about sex.

remember when you liked my poems?
when they made you laugh and cry and you told me you were going to keep them with you despite having so many books sent you, because you liked them so much?

I remember.

You know what's funny?

[this is where on the phone I pause so you can say, "no, tell me what's funny" but we are not on the phone so why am I pausing?]

I didn't know how hot you were back then.
(looks aren't important!)
I didn't know how hot you were but I fell in love with you anyway.
(I thought you were just a normal amount of hot, like the kind a person/woman can deal with without having to *think about it* or *work at it* or whatever)

you were just a normal amount of hot and you were the most interesting person I knew
and you were writing me letters and you were always

so mysterious
and then *finally* you called me – or *finally* I picked up,
and I remember it was the Monday after the weekend
of my birthday
which I now know was the weekend after your
birthday
and my (read: our) birthday had been on a Friday
and mine was the worst I'd ever had (I was really
miserable!)
I didn't know how yours was cuz I didn't know to ask
(cuz you never told me!)
But then you called me the Monday following and
your voice was so sexy
And you were so sweet and I walked all around my
house the fifteen minutes
we were on the phone because I was so nervous,
walking in and out of every room,
my dog following, trying to determine what was
wrong with me...

And immediately after we hung up
I danced and danced and danced!

I danced in and out of every room in this house (the
one I didn't burn down) (the dog following me)

I danced and danced and then I went for a walk that
felt like more dancing ...

It was the worst birthday I could remember and now
I was so happy.

And I didn't even know how hot you were (it didn't/
doesn't matter)

SADDEST POEM

I never knew I was 'his girl'
Til I heard her refer to me as such

Always before – for eighteen months -
        I had wondered
But dared not think of myself as such
(I was always so *careful* to remind everyone we were
'just good friends')

And now here I was
Sobbing on my bedroom floor
Because finally I was 'his girl'
But I only knew because a woman I didn't know was
saying he had to
'clean shit up with *his girl* [me]' on her IG Live thing.

ROCK STAR

There's no amount of $$$ you could offer me
       To shut my mouth
       (unless it was a million; I would maybe shut
it for a million. Dollars. Dineros. Whatever.)
       (and by 'you' I mean the literary community;
don't flatter yourself)

I pay my own bills at The Plaza, Chateau, et al. FYI
       I don't know if I have a sensitive gag reflex
or not
       I've never been very interested in finding
out, tbh
       (what abt U?)

Control your bitch
       Is the best line Axl Rose ever wrote
       Even if there was no way Kurt (or anyone
else) was ever going to control
       Courtney

I've never required a mentor
       I created this monster
       By piecing back together
       The shards of my heart
       (some are sharper than others; sorry!)

you being mad is ok/means you don't own me (either)

(and by 'you': I mean myself)
(don't flatter yourself)
(not everything is about *you*)
(and by 'you' I mean me again so shut the fuck up
already ok?)

walking on eggshells is something I did once
       I didn't care for it TBH

I learned to put cigarettes out on my arm
instead
(it's not that hard)
(is this a poem? Is this punk rock?)

all I really want is to have axl rose think I'm a bitch
or someone who can be controlled
(did something I say make you think that,
honey?)
(and by 'honey' I mean *every member of the
literary community*; don't flatter yourself.)

LANCE ARMSTRONG

I turned on the radio while brushing my teeth
It was set to the FM sports station –
Sometimes I liked to hear the sound of men's voices
Now that I was living alone full time

They were posing a question to their listeners
To elicit calls and texts

The question was regarding Lance Armstrong

When I thought of Lance Armstrong I thought of
Sheryl Crowe
When I thought of Sheryl Crowe I thought of Kid
Rock
That song they sang together

The question was: is *Lance Armstrong a bad person
who did good things
Or a good person who did bad things*

The overwhelming (ly cynical) conclusion was that
Lance Armstrong was a bad person
Who did good things

"He's a narcissist," the sports radio guy said

The day before they'd been talking about Michael
Jordan (doc)
I wondered how anyone could be a GOAT and not
be a narcissist
I wondered how a guy on a sports radio talk show
could talk
Without being a narcissist

I wondered how anyone on social media
Or the internet

Could exist without being an narcissist

Maybe I was just sour
Since I'd been called a narcissist
So frequently
In recent years

Ever since I published a book

Ever since I published two books

Every since I published three books

Ever since I published four books

Who the fuck

Did I think

I was

Who the hell

Did I think

I am

How was Lance Armstrong a narcissist
And not Michael Jordan

How could Sheryl Crowe date
Two known narcissists

Was it possible Sheryl Crowe was a
Narcissist, too?

How could you own an iPhone in America
In 2020 without being a narcissist

MGK

for Colson

I felt dead inside now all the time
Unless I was looking at Machine Gun Kelly online
And then I felt alive
(Alive in the way that makes you want to get a bunch
of tattoos, I mean)

I did everything in life backwards
I figured getting tattoos was just one more example
of this
(getting tattoos underground during quarantine, I
mean)

I felt dead inside
Reading other ppl's poems
Abt leaves and the sky and rain and mammals who
roam the earth
Idgaf abt nature
Like that
Idgaf abt nature in general
I can't imagine writing a poem
Abt nature!

I only felt alive watching MGK videos
While drunk in my basement
Sitting on my basement floor

I only felt alive reading poems that didn't fuck w
Nature

I went for a walk
I was listening to the new song by
Megan thee Stallion and Beyonce
I saw someone (a feminist) had tweeted something
about Beyonce's rapping skills
I heard on the radio Jay Z and The-Dream had helped
Beyonce write her rap lyrics

I wanted to believe Beyonce could write her own
lyrics
I misheard one of the lyrics as "now watch me sweep
up these earrings"
I liked the line so much I was going to use it as an
epigraph for my story collection
Until I got home and googled it and it wasn't anything
abt
Sweeping up earrings

I only feel alive reading/listening to
Ppl from Ohio
I googled MGK and saw he did an annual concert
In the small town in Ohio where I'd grown up
surrounded by
Amish ppl and regular ppl who had icicles in their
bedrooms in winter

I only felt alive while thinking abt
Driving around the rural Ohio shitholes where I'd
grown up
All the hills and streams and cows and manure ...
Shit, man, I just wrote a poem abt nature

Fuck, I don't know how to not feel dead inside
I guess this is why/when ppl start getting tatted up
I guess this is why/when ppl start listening to/fucking
w MGK

I guess this is my life now

Drinking in my basement
And thinking of what new tattoo I'll get next
While fucking w MGK

Untitled love poem/bumfuck michigan

It's impossible to write a love poem
Without sounding like a dick
Without sounding like you've had a lobotomy
Without sounding like cliché words written on
mediocre art at a small midwestern art festival
Somewhere In bumfuck Michigan

The unspecificity of your own stupid romance
The general uninterestingness of happiness

It's so much easier to write about abandonment
Disillusionment, self-harm, separateness

The specificity of getting fucked three times in one
night
By a stranger from bumble who wants you to be his
girl
Who thinks it sounds glamorous or exotic to date a
writer
Who can't possibly know the loneliness of said
endeavor
Until the fourth time he asks if he can come over, the
fourth time you tell him no

Has anyone ever written a truly great poem about
love?
If so, I haven't read it
Better to wait til after the disappointment seeps in,
honey:
My(unsolicited) (writing) advice to you.

Disappointment in yourself, I mean
For all the times you insecurely hid your phone (from
yourself)
All the times you drove right past his house on your
way to a reading
All the times and ways you failed to be the right
woman (for him/for yourself)

Failure is so much more interesting, honey

The irony of coming so many times in one night for
this stranger
When you couldn't come for him
When you wouldn't allow yourself that vulnerability
When standing next to him because you loved him
too much
Because you admired him
Because you're a fucking coward and scared and afraid

Is this a love poem, honey?
I wrote it in ten minutes
Without anyone editing it for me

This is my greatest failure (as a woman): my
independence
My self-alienation, my inability or unwillingness to
Let go my own hand/throat/heart
In order to hold someone else's.

My unwillingness to come for a man I love
(dependence!)
And instead to come for a man I never will (freedom!)

My unwantingness
My wanting and unwanting and wanting again

My stupidity
And my
Self-protection

My liberation
And my defeat.

I can only kill things in with my poems. (I told you
love poems are stupid)

You're welcome. (this poem is my gift to you)

Snitches.

JOE ROGAN (I WAS GOING TO BE SO GREAT)

for David Letterman

I was walking and listening to Joe Rogan again
All I did now was walk and listen to Joe Rogan

It reminded me of the early 90s
When all I did was smoke cigarettes and watch David
Letterman

I didn't know how I would have gotten through my
early 20s
    w/out Letterman (read: *Late Night*) (read:
Kool unfiltereds)
I was a shut in then, too (anxious, panic attack prone,
depressed)

I felt similarly now
How would I get through Covid-19 without Joe
Rogan?

Luckily, I didn't have to

Every day it seemed there was a new Joe Rogan
podcast

And almost every day the new podcast
    Featured a scientist!

I liked listening to scientists (now)
    They soothed and calmed me

Their quiet rational voices
    All their knowledge coming out so quietly
and calmly
    Like a Mr. Rogers' conversation with the
camera while putting on or taking off his shoes

I felt calmed as I did when I was five and watching

Mr. Rogers
I envisioned these scientists wearing cardigans like
Fred also

Mostly I liked listening to Rogan (now)
        Because it was the only place I heard anyone
talking about
        Civil liberties (abt the potential loss of
them, I mean)

No one I knew seemed at all concerned about them
        Everyone I knew seemed happily 'asleep'
watching Netflix shows
        With their families

(Netflix is the opiate of the people!)

I thought, "You know, you could have enforced
family time before Covid-19;
        You could have made your kids eat dinner
with you, help you cook,
        Watch *content* with you without the aid of a
pandemic as an excuse or a reason."

People with families didn't understand there were
people without
        People who were alone, lonely, depressed
        Suicidal; what did they care as long as they
had their
        Families, and Netflix?

What did they care about the loss of civil liberties
        When there were so many new shows on
Netflix
        And they could order their groceries now
for pick up
        When they could feel safer than they've
ever felt
        Locked inside their houses with their
computers and their children?

It reminded me of people who wanted there to be a
wall built
> Between the U.S. and Mexico
> Safety was the issue there too,
> Wasn't it?
> Fear of others
> How could we know whom to fear?
> Mexicans or an Amazon delivery person or
an old friend come to visit...
> Anyone not us could be dangerous -
> How could we know?
> Best to lock down with our families and
watch Netlix
> While we all lose our civil liberties
> And our friends without families grow
more and more depressed
> Who cares about silly things like personal
freedoms and suicidal depression
> When THE VIRUS might get us?

Sometimes I listened to other podcasts
I listened to Katie Couric, too, sometimes

Katie had on a man who was a former surgeon general
> Under Obama
The former Obama surgeon general had made
loneliness
> His platform, after touring the country and
discovering ppl were lonely
> (who knew?!)
Loneliness, he found, was the reason for so much
suffering:
> Opioid addiction, alcoholism, mass
shootings, ... you name it
> The common denominator: people were
lonely

I listened to the former surgeon general talk about
loneliness and then I listened

To a new Joe Rogan podcast

I was extending my walks now
I was walking farther than I ever had just so I could
keep listening
It was good to hear someone else (read: not me) talk
(read: I was lonely)

The person Joe Rogan was talking to was another
scientist
        (Of course!)
the scientists were all running together in my head
now:
there was the one who brought his guitar and sang a
song he'd written
        about war and grandfathers and love
there was the one who wore a mask onto the show
        to promote wearing masks
(oh, maybe that was the same scientist, who did both
of those things,
come to think of it; maybe they were all the same
scientist! Maybe I was going crazy
like the lady who thought Letterman was talking
directly to her every night
through her television set)

I didn't think Joe Rogan was speaking directly to me
        Through my carbuds
I didn't have dreams about him, either, as I had
Letterman
        In the early 90s
        (read: I didn't think he was sexy)
        (Letterman had been so sexy!)

He was just someone to listen to
        Who had a sense of humor
I decided I'd chosen the wrong profession
        I decided I should have been a comedian
        So I could hang out with other comedians,
        So *everything* would be funny (even the loss

of civil liberties!)
        Instead of self-accusatory and self-loathing
and self-vilifying

I wondered if it were too late
        To start a whole new career
        To 'build a set'
I wondered how long it would take me to get on Joe
Rogan
        If I started writing my set now
        If I practiced and practiced
        While locked down under quarantine
        While locked out of my best friend's house

eventually, as always happens, I had to stop walking
(at some point)
I went back to my garage, took off my boots and
winter jacket (it was snowing in april!)
And went inside.

I stood in front of my mirror
        I had a whole bit already worked out about
dolphins being rapists
        And preteen girls having posters of dolphins
on their bedroom walls
surrounded by hearts and rainbows and smiley faces
        becuz they didn't know about the dolphins
        And their raping.
But *I knew*, cuz I used to listen to NPR
        And one morning a young female scientist
had talked about dolphins
        How a male dolphin or group of male
dolphins would sidle up to a female dolphin
        Kidnap her, swim her away from the group
(pod?)
        Even if she had a kid (name for dolphin
infant?)
        They'd just bring her kid along too
        When they swam her away and raped her

This was something I'd learned on NPR
Back before I listened to Joe Rogan
I'd listened to scientists, then, too

Maybe I just really had a thing for scientists
            I wondered if it were too late
            To start a whole new career
I was always wondering things like this
            But then I was always just a writer
            Same shit, different day [SAMO!].
            Virus or no virus:
            It was always the same. (read: I was always
the same)

I wasn't ever going to be on Joe Rogan or NPR
I was always going to be lonely because I didn't know
how not to be
            An asshole.
It was the one thing I was really good at
            So maybe I could be a comedian, after all.
I got out a pen and started working on my dolphin
material
            Started working on my life-as-an-asshole
material.
            Started working.

I got so busy I forgot to wash my hands
            Forgot to buy Clorox wipes
            Forgot to check how many deaths there'd
been in my state in the past 24 hours.

I was going to be a comedian now
            If only in my own house, in my basement
            Like Robert De Niro's character in The
King of Comedy
            Like a guy I heard abt once on NPR who
had a whole late night set in his living room

I would interview scientists in my garage
I would interview aged rock stars and aged actresses

and most of the other ageds
I was going to have my own channel on YouTube
I was going to talk about how I was censored and a rebel and a free thinker!

I was going to be delusional now on top of being an asshole
It was going to be so great! I was about to be so great!
I had extended my dolphin-rapist bit by thirty seconds -
I was going to be so great.

ELIZABETH ELLEN

Baby, I put my own name on my body/tshirt/purse/
poems
Does that make me a narcissist, babe?

Well, which is it, baby? Narcissism or using you for
your name?

I'll answer:
I only use my own name for the advancement self-
destruction (of my career)

Unlike anyone on social media sites
Unlike -----

I'm not Sid and Nancy
Im Sid

I'm not Mickey and Mallory
I'm Mallory

I'm not Kurt and Courtney
I'm whichever fucking one of them I want to be in
the moment

I'm not Keith Hernandez
I'm Elizabeth Ellen

You used to like this about me
Remember, babe?

you used to like everything about me
(even if there was never really any room for you here
in these killing fields)

most especially (you liked): my name!

KANYE WEST

Twenty-five years earlier I'd been in a Laundromat
In Columbus
Ohio

This was, what,
1992, 1993?

I was just another dumb white girl
From a small town in Ohio
BFE
Bum fuck Egypt
We called it then

Sometimes you said BMI
Butt fuck India

Bum fuck
Butt fuck
I don't know

We were just dumb white people

None of us had ever been to India
Or Egypt – much less knew where they were
On a map

I was just another dumb white girl
who liked Spike Lee movies
who thought Wesley Snipes in *Jungle Fever*
was hot

who'd fucked a black football player
at ASU
in Tempe
when my best white girlfriend was dating a
black football player too

the black football player whose name I still remember

but won't use here out of respect for him
was the second person to make me come

he was the first person I knew who wore a do-rag

he made me come a lot

that one spring break, that one summer after

whenever I flew to Arizona to see my friend

I probably could have fallen in love with him
If we ever saw each other in daylight
I was probably just another dumb white girl to him

but back to the Laundromat
some four or five years later
after I'd watched some Spike Lee movies
after I'd gone to see Spike Lee give a lecture
at THE Ohio State University

I was there on a Saturday afternoon washing my
clothes
My white Republican golfer boyfriend was at work
at the
Golf shop down the street

There was a black man in the Laundromat doing his
Wash too
The old lady who ran the Laundromat was white
(very) old and (very) white

She waited til the young black man had left the
Laundromat
To make a disparaging comment about him
I don't remember for sure
But she probably used the n-word

She was talking to another white person
 Not me

I went home and got my red velvet ball cap,
A piece of paper and a marker
I wrote on the piece of white paper:
RACISM IS UN-AMERICAN
I cut a circle around the words,
Taped the circle to my hat

I drove back to the Laundromat
Wearing the red velvet hat
I didn't say a word
Just stood there taking my clothes out of the dryer,
Folding them

I was shy
I was scared of confrontation

If someone had a pro-life sticker on their car
I wrote a note, left it under their windshield

I fumed silently

I don't remember if the old white lady saw my hat
What she said or how she reacted if she did
If anyone else in the Laundromat saw it

It was such a microscopic gesture

Vs the whole wide world of racism

I thought I wasn't racist because I'd fucked
A black guy
Cuz he'd made me come

Cuz I wrote words on a hat

Cuz I watched Spike Lee movies

Cuz I listened to Public Enemy, Snoop Dogg,
En Vogue, Young M.C.

I thought I wasn't racist cuz I saw *Poetic Justice* in the theater
Cuz I wanted to look like Janet Jackson on the cover of *Rolling Stone*
Cuz I thought Tupac was sexy
Cuz I thought Tupac was smart

I was just another dumb white girl from BFE Ohio

I am just another dumb white girl

Who got excited July 4th, 2020
When Kanye announced he was running for president

Twenty-five years and so little change

Twenty-five years and still so many dumb white girls.

Twenty-five years later and I think listening to Beyonce makes me
Not a racist.

Anyway, I voted for Ye.
POST MALONE

[redacted]
[redacted[
[redacted]

Have you noticed I've been so careful in this poem with pronouns
Until now I have been so careful not to use 'you' or 'he' or 'him'
I am so careful!

[fellatio is still 'not punk' – *why can't you remember this?*]

I just want to be the man in white face ~~dancing~~

thrashing around on stage while Nirvana plays Breed at Reading

I just want to be the woman jumping up and down/ jogging in place slightly offstage to Breed in Live! Tonight! Sold out!!

I don't think there's a single person wearing makeup in the audience of Nirvana's Unplugged concert [spoiler: they don't play Breed; maybe that's why nobody dances]

#mid90s!

[cunnilingus is still 'punk' - *how many times do I have to remind you of this?!*]

I am done being careful:

-My hair is thinning and/or falling out and/or I am going crazy
-I have a 5.6 centimeter fibroid tumor in my abdomen and/or I am crazy and/or my hair is falling out
-I think I might have an anal flap also
(I bet you had to google 'anal flap')
(maybe it's just a hemorrhoid)
(does that make me prettier?)
(ok)

I just want to dance on stage barefooted in a tie while Kurt Cobain ~~sings~~ wails

(who wants to feel it? my fibroid, I mean. Or my anal flap, either one)

Do you think Courtney ever had her heart broken?
Aside from Kurt dying, I mean.
Do you think Courtney ever had an anal flap, I mean?
I never had my heart broken I was just wondering!

(you can feel it - my fibroid, I mean - through my abdomen if I lie down flat on the floor)
(it's not like a baby but it's not *not* like a baby!)
(you can sing a song to it, I mean, like, maybe, Breed)
(I don't know anyone who wants to feel my anal flap but I'm confident *someone* will *sometime*)

I am done being careful:

-two nights a week I drink five or six shots of 100 proof whiskey and smoke 10 or 11 cigarettes
-I barely make it up the stairs
-thank god my daughter is too old (read: could not care less) to hang around and video me eating a burger off the carpet
-the room just spins and spins and spins (but I am ok!) (I am done being careful!)

I just want to get thrown off stage by security while Kurt Cobain sings
I just want to get thrown out of a reading for smoking a Benson & Hedges cigarette
I just want to get thrown out of anywhere I might dare to show up in a hospital gown
I just want ~~you~~ Post Malone to finger me while singing ~~Breed~~ Heart-Shaped Box and smoking with his other hand

(my hemoglobin level is 7.4 – is that sexy?)
(if I have to have a blood transfusion will that make me sexier pour vous?)
I just want to be sexy! (pour ~~vous~~ Post Malone!)

The other night I was pretty sure I could feel my liver through my abdomen
Like Richard Burton's when his was enlarged
But maybe I am just dumb, I think I'm just dumb

I just want to smoke Post Malone's cigarette with my ~~vagina twat~~ pussy on that counter   behind him like a woman in Amsterdam while he sings Heart-Shaped Box (again)

(who wants to pay to watch my blood being transfused?)
(who wants to pay to watch me eat a burger off the carpet?)
(who wants to go to White Castle and get me a burger?)
(I only eat White Castle now, ~~I'm sorry~~)

Also I am just like Kurt

Just, like, I can't eat and my stomach hurts

Just, like, I want my wife to give me a blowjob every morning before we get out of bed

Just, like, I have everything I've ever wanted (read: ~~you~~) and I'm still sad (~~sorry!~~)

Just, like, everyone is gay, I think I'm gay now, I can't deal w ~~men~~ anyone now

Just, like, *I don't care I don't care I don't care I don't care I don't care care care if it's old*

Just, like, I can't deal with anyone anymore if your name's not Post Malone now

Just, like, I want to care as little what I look like as Post Malone (when his face is puffy and red and there's a wall of pretty pretty alcohol-filled bottles behind him) now

Am I pretty? Somebody please tell me I am pretty

Is this punk rock? Somebody please tell me this is punk rock

KELLY BUNDY (July, 2020)

for N.S.

A few days after our first date you sent me a text
You were the first guy I'd dated in eighteen years
who wasn't a writer

The text said, "I just read one of your poems on the
internet
And I liked it!!!"

You sent me another text after that one that said, "I
don't know why you didn't want me to read your
writing on the internet!!"

Earlier I'd sent you a picture of my picture on the
back of one of my books
And you'd said, "I'm going to need a lot more pictures
like that!!"

I liked you because you weren't a writer
Or I liked a lot of things about you and one was that
you weren't a writer
(another was you gave good head)

I didn't like to think too much about writing anymore
I didn't like feeling like a member of a cult anymore,
either

I said I'd write a poem for you
So you could google me and read about yourself

I said I'd wear the fishnets like in the book photo
The next time you came over
I told you I had a leather jacket,
Leather motorcycle boots...the works!

You said, "Hot, you'll look like Kelly Bundy."

I liked how easy it was to please you;
How easily you fucked me.

I didn't have to wait and wait and wait.
Weeks or months or years or never (like with writers).

I said the poem I'm writing about you is going to be
called
"Kelly Bundy."

Some people didn't like to be written about
But you didn't seem to mind

You seemed to think it was cool or glamorous
or some shit -
Dating a writer

Mostly we just watched videos on YouTube of exotic
animals -
And the crazy men who bought and sold them -
Between fucking

Sometimes we stood out on my balcony watching the
deer
And you'd be behind me
And you'd wrap your arm around me
Cover my mouth with your hand
"Shhhhhh," you'd tell me

and I'd laugh and ask, "Did you just shhhhhush me?"
and you'd nod and say, "Shhuuuush."
And cover my mouth back up again with your hand

I really liked this about you most
How you weren't afraid to shush me
How you covered my mouth with your hand.

I like this and I liked how you fucked me;
Even though I kept forgetting to wear the damn
fishnets.

Even though I didn't look anything like Kelly Bundy.
Even though, even though.

S. E. Hinton (June, 2020)

for N.S.

I hadn't fucked in eighteen months and finally I was
fucking
Earlier we'd gone to a restaurant for pizza
The pizza was the white kind, not red
We'd picked the one with sausage and peppers
Without paying much attention to what type of
peppers

When the waiter brought the pizza each slice had
One tiny round piece of sausage on it
And about a zillion large peppers

I'm not eating all those peppers, I said
Me either, you said

We each ate maybe one pepper
There were still a billion peppers on the tray
When the waiter returned to take it

Do you want a box, the waiter asked
I wasn't sure if this was some kind of joke
If the waiter was trying to be funny
No thanks, I said
You were shaking your head
The waiter was wearing a mask

Earlier, when I'd parked the car outside the restaurant
You'd patted your pockets
Oh shit, you'd said, I forgot my mask in my car
Fortunately I had a stack in my console
You can wear one of these, I said
You looked at them all and chose the one with
cherries on it
I made a point of not looking at you
Until we were seated and you'd taken the mask off
Not on account of the cherries, but, idk, just because

After dinner we were on my couch in the basement
We'd sat on the basement carpet in front of the TV
Side by side
Looking through my DVDs for ten minutes
Now we were watching a young Matt Dillon
And a medium young Mickey Rourke
And a very young Nicolas Cage

Did you pick this movie because you knew Nicolas
Cage is in it, I said
You'd told me people told you you look like Nicolas
Cage

You shook your head
I didn't know nicolas cage was in it, you said
It didn't matter if I believed you
I was smiling
We were laughing; you looked a little like Nic Cage

Earlier you'd been standing on my balcony talking to
me
With an unlit cigarette dangling from your mouth

You were talking about deer or deer-hunting or
something
Something:
Working in an automobile factory...
dating auto show girls ...
vicodin addiction ...
how Kid Rock was an asshole ...
Something.

I couldn't hear you because I was staring at your
mouth
Thinking how hot it was when you talked with a
cigarette dangling from it

Now we were watching Rumble Fish and you had
your arm around me

And you were playing with my nipple
You played with my nipple during the whole couch
scene
With Diane Lane and Matt Dillon
Pretty soon we weren't watching Rumble Fish
anymore
Even though Matt Dillon as Rusty James was really
cute
Even though there was a nerdy character stand in for
the author,
For S. E. Hinton, who followed Rusty James around
and wrote
Shit down in a notebook while everyone else rumbled

You were kissing me and my underwear was off and I
was just wearing
My short denim skirt and my short denim skirt was
up

Earlier I'd cried for two hours worrying how this
would go
If I'd be able to fuck
Or to get fucked
Or if everything would work right
Since I hadn't had sex in eighteen months
Since I hadn't had sex with anyone but one person
In eighteen years

You did stuff and other stuff and more stuff and then
you entered me
When you entered me it hurt like hell
It hurt like the first time
Like losing your virginity (like the Madonna song)
Even though I couldn't remember losing my virginity
If it'd hurt or not
Since I'd been drunk on wine coolers
That first time

I wasn't drunk the other night when you fucked me
though

And it hurt like hell the first time but I didn't let on
I was just so happy to be fucking (you)/to be getting
fucked
I was just so grateful to have you (a dick) inside me

The second time – an hour later – it hurt way less
And I came really hard and you came and Matt Dillon
wasn't on the TV anymore
We smoked on the balcony after and the neighbors
were staring really hard
I wasn't wearing any underwear under my short white
denim skirt
I felt a little like Sharon Stone in the interrogation
scene in Basic Instinct
The way I smoked my cigarette, the way I rested my
feet, one atop the other,
On the balcony railing

You fucked me again after we smoked,
you fucked me one more time
Before you had to make the hour long drive
back to the east side of the state
back to your job at the Ford plant
where you've worked the last twenty years
where you take a shower sometimes before driving
an hour west to ~~see~~ fuck me.

After which I write notes in my notebook
Like Rusty James' nerdy friend in Rumble Fish
Like the character we made fun of
Before you fucked me for the first time Monday night
Like the character stand in for the author
Like S. E. Hinton.

another shithole poem I'll never publish (7-29-2020)

My boyfriend is convinced I'm still in love with you
Because of the cigarette burns on my arm
He asked me when I did them and I said last winter
and he said why
I said I wanted to know what it would feel like; how
bad it could hurt
I said I wanted to know if I was as fucked up as a man,
as fucked up as you

I said, no, no, I swear I'm not
I promise you
I'm not still in love with him

We were standing on my balcony, staring at a group
of deer,
He behind me, his arms forming boundaries on either
side as he gripped the railing in front

I wasn't lying
When I said it
I meant every word

I wasn't still in love with you
Two weeks ago
I swear
I swear

Even if the way he smokes a cigarette
Occasionally reminds me of you

Even if

I wasn't lying

I wasn't still in love with you

I just liked the way the scars looked on the inside of
my arm

How they reminded me of our friendship...
How you said it was important we always be friends

You probably weren't lying then, either
You probably meant every word, at the time

Did you show him? He asked me
Yeah, I said. I showed him
What did he say?
He showed me his . . .
But I promise you: I'm not still in love with him
Stop worrying, baby, I promise

Then today I watched a video of your npr interview
I don't know why I did that
That was a stupid thing to do

Because it showed a prison cell and I didn't know if it
was your actual
Prison cell or just one that looked like it

Either way it made me cry
It made me bawl
staring at the prison cell while listening to your voice

That soft, slow drawl
That I remembered . . .

And I thought of the months we were writing letters
The months you were reading my books
While I was reading ----
The phone calls...
Your soft slow drawl making me laugh,
Telling me 'take care'
Before we were cut off again; another month to wait

I bawled because I didn't understand which one of us
was lying
The one of us who said she's not still in love with you
Or the one of us who said it was important we always
remain friends

Guns n Roses (September, 2020)

for N.S. – Happy Birthday!!!

I didn't write a poem abt you in August;
I'm sorry, we were just so busy fucking
And doing *other stuff* ...

Other stuff like meeting in hotels with heart-shaped
hot tubs
And motels with hookers and drug dealers outside
And hotels with syringes on the ground
And people in folding chairs barbequing in the
parking lot

We played 20 Q's and Truth or Truth
Because we were too lazy/comfortable for dares
And one of the questions was "will you marry me"
And I said you can't joke abt shit like that
And you said ok what if I told you I love you
And I said you can't joke abt shit like that either
Or maybe I didn't say anything
 I remember kissing you and I remember
Uma Thurman was on the motel TV;
It was Kill Bill Vol Two
We'd already watched Vol One in the hot tub

We didn't know we had Chlamydia yet
We would find that out the next day
Or a week later
I forget which

I don't remember when I said I love you back, either
Maybe a few days later
Maybe sooner
I don't think I said it that night
I don't think I knew I loved you til you told me you
loved me

Anyway ...

I woke up this morning thinking
I'm so glad my bf isn't a writer!
i woke up this morning thinking
I have to write my bf a birthday poem!

But first I bought us tickets to a guns n roses concert
That doesn't even take place til next summer
Which seems wildly optimistic of me
And sort of counter to what I always seem to be
telling you ...

How I'm a liberated woman
How independence is important to me
How I don't ever again want to feel not liberated/free
...

When we met on Bumble I said I was just looking for
a casual fling
Someone to fuck once a week or so
Someone to hang out and play gin with when we're
not fucking
You said, didn't you see on my profile - how
I said I was looking for a serious relationship?
Oh sure, I said, I saw -
But I just ignored that

we both laughed because we were each ignoring
What the other was saying
We just kept fucking each other like there was no
disagreement
On how our future would go

Then there was the night you drove over without
telling me
I got back from a walk with the dog and there you
were –
In my driveway!

I just had to see you, you said

I've never felt like this about anyone, you told me
You were on your knees on my front porch,
And I was sitting in my chair, smoking a cigarette ...

I wanted to be mad at you –
I tried to avoid looking at you -
I was really pissed when I first saw your car
In my drive

I'm a strong, independent woman! I thought
who does this guy think he is? I asked myself –
Ignoring everything I've told him!

But then I looked at you
And your face was soft with emotion
Here you were, a big strong man who works
In an auto factory,
On your knees in front of me
Asking me for something –
I wasn't sure what

And before I knew it I wasn't pissed anymore
I was in your lap
My mouth pressed to your cheek ...

I'm a strong, independent woman
In love with a strong, passionate man
Who reminds me of a character
In a Tennessee Williams' play
Who reminds me of a Marlon Brando character –
Smoking in a wife beater,
Crying on my porch -
Who reminds me every day
I'm in love with him;
That it's ok to be strong and independent
And in love!

And if the end of the world happens
Next summer
I want to be with two people:

I want to be with you and axl rose!

Anyway, happy birthday, baby

This poem doesn't rhyme, either

I hope that's okay

I know you like rhyming poems

But anyway, i don't know how to rhyme.

I don't know much, actually.

I know I love you.
I know I'm so happy we both got on Bumble,
And that you asked me out right away,
Before anyone else asked me,
Before you met that girl in Canada ...
Because I love you I love you I love you.
And not much rhymes with Canada.

(the) Conjuring

As a new hobby, I think about sabotaging our relationship. I think about this a lot while we're at Home Depot looking at Christmas lights.

"If we ended it right now, think about how good it would end," I say.

You look at me funny when I say this. We are each buying a new Dustbuster, tho for some reason yours costs twenty dollars more than mine.

"I don't get you, baby, why would you say shit like that?" you say, your mask under your nose. "If you want to break up with me, just do it; get it over with."

But that's not what I'm saying at all.

I spend another twenty minutes after dinner fantasizing about ending things. You come in from smoking and playing video games on my front porch and I'm crying and crying. I thought you'd left. "I'm just so tired," I say. I am apologetic. (I am your baby, your baby girl.)

I hide my eyes with your hands. An hour ago you wanted me to dominate you. Thigh highs, cock ring, handcuffs. You can't get more All-American than that.
When you come inside me you say: shit, goddamn, fuck.
When you come inside I say, "We better break up now," and I am crying and crying.

another Denis Johnson ER story

It was almost a year to the day of my last ER visit
i knew now where to go –
front desk, guy w blood pressure machine, hallway
bench, blood test

i sat in the waiting area after all that, waiting and
trying not to think
about covid19
everyone in the waiting area was visibly trying not to
think abt covid19
we were all doing ok
all of us except the older woman in the wheelchair
the older woman in the wheelchair started yelling,
*Hello? hello? I've been here three hours, I'm in pain, I
have an open wound!*
a nurse glanced over
Yes, ma'am, the nurse said
but the nurse didn't do anything. no one did anything
the old woman just sat in her wheelchair, holding her
side
while i tried to determine if she was crazy or had an
open wound or
If she was crazy *and had* an open wound, whatever

time passed and i stopped trying to determine things
that went double for my own problems
path of least resistance, i told myself multiple times
a day
that worked okay most of the time
i barely drank anymore
i kept thinking "sit and drink pennyroyal tea" while
smoking
on my porch with a mug of chamomile

someone had accused me of being a drunk
i didn't mind
i would be whatever anyone wanted me to be
i had been a rape apologist, I'd been cancelled

i would be a drunk also

path of least resistance
90s apathy; *whatever, bro*

i was at the ER because i couldn't take the burning
anymore
it burned like shit every time I pissed and sometimes
when i didn't
sometimes my vagina just burned for no good reason

i'd gone to the urgent care by my house five days
before, pissed in a plastic cup,
had a greasy-haired doctor touch my pelvis
you don't have a UTI, he said
he sent my piss out to a lab for further testing
further testing was a polite way of saying STDs

back in July i'd had Chlamydia
oh, I'd had yeast, too
i'd fucked a lot and this was my comeuppance
for all that Detroit motel fucking
the heart-shaped hot tubs
the greasy briskets after ...
the cigarettes and the cigarettes and the cigarettes

but that was in July and now it was December
and it burned, burned, burned again and again and
again
(comeuppance!)
path of least resistance had led me to the ER
i didn't have health insurance
i didn't have a general practitioner
i didn't have a gynecologist

i had a fibroid the size of a small orange (shout out
FKA twigs!)
and low hemoglobin (could I sue somebody, too?!)
i had a boyfriend i liked to fuck
despite the fibroid and the low hemoglobin

the Chlamydia and the yeast

we still fucked anyway
even tho I burned
i texted him a photo of my arm w the blood thing in it
i texted him while he was still at work –
afternoon shift, millwright, auto plant
(he could have been a pipefitter! – he'd told me once,
late at night, phone sex'ing)
i was in my own room by then –
a room with a bed and a TV and a remote
like a motel in Detroit but much more expensive
i had white blood cells in my urine,
my hemoglobin was lower than it'd ever been!
earlier that morning i'd considered climbing the stairs
to the second floor
it'd felt like considering climbing a mountain
or at the very least a tall hill
i was tired as fuck, is what I mean
i didn't know how i was going to wrap all those
Christmas presents,
how i was going to host guests
how i was going to keep fucking my coulda-been-a-
pipefitter! bf

I lay in the hospital bed changing channels
that show w Andy Griffith was on
i can never remember If It's called the Andy Griffith
show
or Mayberry r.f.d.
maybe those were two diff shows
from my childhood
i don't know, i can't remember

i lay there watching Andy Griffith with the tv muted
thinking,
maybe i have cancer
i remember thinking i was 'ok w it'
everyone i knew was freaking out about the
coronavirus

my mom drove all the way from florida to ohio and
then turned around and drove back
i didn't get it
i felt ok w dying
not, like, suicidal
not like i gave a shit what ppl thought of me
(if i ever start caring what anyone in the literary
community thinks of me,
someone please shoot me)
more like i'm really fucking tired and I'm not scared
of dying
path of least resistance

but i didn't have cancer
or if i do they haven't found it yet
i just had a really bad UTI that somehow evaded the
greasy-haired doctor
at urgent care
and yeast
i always always have yeast

i'd been in the ER seven hours
and hadn't eaten a thing
the young cute nurse went and got me a turkey
sandwich
all the female nurses were young and cute
i'm sorry if that's a stereotype
sometimes stereotypes are true
she was young and cute and handed me my turkey
sandwich
with my pills on the side like a movie w winona ryder
and angelina jolie
and i fantasized they weren't antibiotics and
antifungals
i fantasized I was a pill popper
a valley of the dolls babe

like my bf's BM
like my bf used to be before he got on the stuff they
give you

to get off the kind of pills you eat

why am i am so boring

on the drive home –
after I gave the valet ten dollars for working a shitty job
during a pandemic –
i turned on the radio
it was turned to the classic rock station
now classic rock was everything i'd ever listened to before turning forty
all music -according to me – was classic rock
i turned on the classic rock station and got on the highway
i didn't want to go home yet
i was still so fucking tired
but I wanted to go somewhere
i decided I'd go to mcdonald's
even tho it was ten pm and a week night and the middle of a pandemic
Bush's "Come Down" was playing
i'd never gave a shit about Bush one way or the other
whenever i thought of gavin rossdale I thought of gwen stefani
i thought, i wonder what plastic surgery she's had
but now the music was moving me somehow
like all bad 90s music moves me if the time is right
if I'm driving the freeway alone at night
I was already going 90, i inched higher to 100
and then 110 and then 115
the five mph between 115 and 120 are harder
my body started shaking w adrenaline
i was so boring

"i don't wanna come back down from this cloud"

i kept going – i was ok w getting cancer or covid19
i was ok w crashing as long as that was it
i didn't want to live in a wheelchair

i didn't want to have to have plastic surgery
i was asking a lot, i know

"*this cloud, this cloud, this cloud,
this cloud, this cloud, this cloud,
this cloud, this cloud, this cloud*"

i was texting all that – *all the this clouds* – into my
phone notes
while i was driving 115mph
getting ready to drive 120
i was typing "i was ok w it" too
meaning all of it
this, that, the other ...
everything.

this is a poem or a tweet or an ig post

one time warren beatty was in a documentary abt
Madonna

warren beatty said why *would she want to live off
camera?* (I am paraphrasing) *There's nothing to say
off camera. What would be the point? Why exist, off
camera?*

Kanye Couch

We were sitting on my new white couch
Destiny called it a Kanye couch
My daughter said it looked like it should be in a
museum

We were sitting on my Kanye couch and crying
You'd started crying first
You thought I was going to break up w you again

We got in my bed and I kept asking you politely to
fuck me
It'd been three days since I went to the ER
You said you were worried abt hurting me
You fucked me but you wouldn't cum inside me

I was still on antibiotics
It was almost xmas

When am I going to see you again? you said
We were on my porch, smoking
The xmas lights you'd hung weeks earlier, shining

One of the first stories you ever told me
Was abt hanging out backstage at a kid rock show
And ray liotta talking to you
I forgot, now, what ray liotta said

Your BM was fucking kid rock or kid rock wanted
Her around, after, at his parties

In the summer when we met you wore wife beaters
And everyone said you looked like nicolas cage
When I showed them our pictures

the day the Kanye couch arrived
I'd gotten my hair done
The man who came to the door to deliver it said,
"I like your hair" and stared a while at my feet

I wasn't wearing any shoes
And my toenails were painted blue
I wasn't wearing a mask, either

You said, "of course he wanted to fuck you"
When I told you the thing he said

I lay on my Kanye couch after he left
Taking photos for you

It felt like a museum

It was the middle of summer and I hadn't met your
son yet

I hadn't been backstage at a kid rock concert
I hadn't met ray liotta

There were so many things I hadn't done

Please read dennis cooper rn please

Remember when you could watch a movie liked
Badlands
w/out worrying abt the moral choices of the
characters
or how old the girl was (14) (to his 20 – aghast!
Clutch pearls!)
when you watched a film for the beauty of the
cinematography
the indieness of the soundtrack
the cool style of the actor/actress/horses

remember when Jodie foster played a twelve year old
prostitute
when she was twelve?
She turned out alright, huh?
I mean, who amongst us turned out 'alright,' anyway?

Remember when jim carroll made money for drugs
By turning tricks in nyc when he was fifteen
Sucking guys' dicks, letting them suck his
So he could score some dope
Remember when one of the ramones did the same
thing (at the same age?)

Remember when my baby daddy impregnated
His high school girlfriend when he was 15 and she
was 16
And a catholic so kept the baby and raised it
And now that baby is 27 and one of the loves of my
life

Remember when my boyfriend's brother's friend
Was 13 and knocked up a 30 year old and his mom
raised the baby
As if it was her own
Like Jack Nicholson's mom/grandma/whatever?

Remember when the fact you could make a baby

Meant you weren't a baby/child, anymore?

Remember how bonnie was sixteen when she married her first husband,
Not clyde?

Remember when it was normal to leave home and move to a new continent
To find work when you were seventeen (Donald trump's grandfather)
To forge a fake ID so you could go to war before you were eighteen???
Remember when kids moved out of their parents' houses
Wanted to drive a car
Wanted to get drunk/fuck/suck cock/do drugs/ worship the devil/runaway
From home/join a commune/cult/band?

Remember when joan jett moved to LA w her parents' permission
At 15 to start a band/make her own money/do WHATEVER she fuckin wanted?

Remember when that was *cool*?

Remember when art was art
And if you bitched abt the morality of it you were part of the
Religious right?
Or a real square?
A total drag, *man*
Pedestrian
Bourgeois
NOT VERY SMART
Not INTEL-ec-tulle

A BORE

Remember when garth greenwell talked about

cruising parks
When he was 14/15, having sex w adult men
Remember how that's ok/how it didn't cause him
trauma
Because all boys wanna fuck
All the time
Always

Like sam lansky
Who wrote a memoir about being a teenaged boy
Fucking older men (and younger men and whoever!)

Nancy Spungen was 20 when she died
She'd already been a stripper and a prostitute
And a runaway at age 17

Courtney love was a runaway and a stripper at age 17

Angelina jolie's mother let angelina's boyfriend
move into the house and live in her bedroom when
Angelina was 14

Melanie Griffith started dating don johnson when he
was 22 and she was 14

If r Kelly had waited five months and he and aaliyah
had been from Canada he would have had no problem
legally fucking her

I was wrong about bonnie parker
She was still 15, six days shy of 16, when she married
roy thornton
She still had a tattoo on her knee with their names
inside a heart
-Bonnie&Roy -
The day she died next to Clyde.

Please read dennis cooper rn please

NEWLYWEDS

I'm already anticipating all the moments
Of locking myself in the bathroom
With a cigarette and
Glass of wine

I'm already anticipating all the times
You will cheat on me
With your ex,
W a woman from high school,
W a woman from a dating app you haven't yet
Been banned from
W a woman your partner in the plant (Jazz) knows

Because of my never-ending need
For alone time in the bathroom

The glass of red wine and cigarette
so damn good
on the toilet seat
Without you

Googling "irritated vulva"
After fucking three times
After your hunting trip
Up north
After viewing your ex
On the steps of her
Double wide:
Cigarette, bronzer, pills
A decade of your life
Before me.

How to Buy Instagram Followers

The first time Nico called me I was pacing my house
With a shot of whiskey, the dog following
My husband still at his campus office
Another hour

It was April, 2019
The Monday after our shared birthday
Tho I didn't know then
We shared a birthday
I barely knew anything, then
Nico was still in prison
the warden – Mr. Nicely - denied me visitation
and I considered burning my house down
There wasn't much else to know

The last time Nico called me I was
Sitting on my porch with a beer and a cigarette
It was just before or just after Thanksgiving, 2020
I forget which

Nico was no longer in prison
I was divorced
Nico was or wasn't yet married
There wasn't much else to know.

TITTIES

I was thinking this morning
About how when your son came in my house
He pointed to the photograph of Miley Cyrus
On the cover of a *Rolling Stone* I had on display
On a magazine rack

"*I know*," you said.
"But she's covering them," you said, meaning her titties.

I was thinking about how
Two nights before
I'd been sitting on the couch with your son
While he watched *Child's Play* for the
Umpteenth time in your living room

It was the scene where the mom realizes Chucky
Doesn't need batteries

It was the scene where Chucky calls the mom
A stupid bitch,
A filthy slut.

You were in the kitchen or bathroom
I got up off the couch

It's not, like, I'm an uptight feminist or anything
But it felt misogynistic even to me,
A seven year old boy idolizing a doll who calls women
Bitches and sluts
Before biting them, before hitting and punching them,
After killing another woman ...

But, hey, at least Miley Cyrus's titties weren't in the movie
For him to see.

HONEYMOON IN VEGAS

I think it's incredibly sexist
When ppl ask
Who paid for the plane tickets
And hotel room
The weekend we eloped
In Vegas.

Like all the jewelry store commercials
Depicting couples on holidays,
Always a man holding out a small velvet-lined box,
Always a woman smiling widely,
Her love paid for, bought:
with diamonds and gold.

I never liked diamonds, anyway.

I like fucking you
Independent of what gem stones you can afford
To buy me.

I just like fucking you, okay?
Why can't anyone get that?

I bought all three of my wedding bands,
So fucking what.

ANNULMENT

What if one day I'm too tired
To leave the bathroom
To eat dinner w you
And your kid

You should have thought of this
When you married a woman
Ten years your senior

With a penchant for wine and cigarettes
And fasting
In the bathroom
Door locked
La Perla gown on the floor
Ashes all around

Women my age go crazy
I told you this
I told you abt the woman I saw on the news in my
youth -
"raking rabbits" on her front lawn,
The age I am now

She'd also killed her family
I think I told you that too

If I lock myself in the bathroom, sweetheart
It's for your own protection,
Not mine

If you see me carrying in a bottle
Don't try and stop me

I'm probably just tired
I'm always so fucking tired now
I'm just so fucking tired.

AMAZON PRIME

I was waiting
I was in my gold dress
The one with the shoulder pads like you like
Joan Collins, Linda Evans, *Dynasty*

I was in my gold dress, waiting for you

It was after the time you normally come home from
work
I hadn't looked at my phone all day
I was terrified of rejection (it was our first big fight,
sleeping in separate beds!)
(I was terrified of you)

There was the sound of wheels, an engine
The dog picked up her head
In synchronicity: we both turned our heads toward
the door
We were eager; a kinder word for desperate
Eager for daddy to get home

I started crying when I saw it was only a Prime van
That it wasn't my husband (you/daddy)

It was a large cardboard box: your Xmas present
I lugged it upstairs in my gold dress, panting

I went back to what I'd been doing before:
Pretending not to listen for cars (your car) while
writing a blurb for a friend.

If you're not here by six I plan to slip my snow pants
on under my gold dress,
Light a cigarette on the front porch,
So very Joan Collins, so very *Dynasty* ...

Do you think Linda Evans ever waited for her
husband to come home in a gold dress and snow

pants?

Do you think Joan Collins ever smoked on the front porch, head downcast, waiting, shamefully for her 'daddy'?

At least your Xmas present is here, anyway.
At least you weren't here when it arrived. (but what if you never do? What if our first big fight is our last? Questions to contemplate in gold lame, in shoulder pads, in snow pants, on the front porch while smoking.)

"I haven't bought drugs in six months," you said

After you left I ran my hand over the toilet lid to feel for residue
I didn't lick my hand; I should have licked my hand
I tasted the suboxone in your mouth, tho, when you kissed me goodbye

I never noticed you taking your backpack everywhere before
You used the bathroom at target last night
You always make sure I lock the car doors now

KIRK WHITE

I asked you while watching Kirk White do lines off
a toilet lid
If it was triggering for you
You were eating one of my homemade brownies with
vanilla ice cream
You were feeding me scoops direct into my mouth

We'd only been married a month, maybe six weeks
I was still so naïve then
I still am

I still don't know how many times you snorted
Narco/Adderall/cocaine
In the bathroom of Target/Barnes/PF Chang's/my
house/your house/wherever

After we got married

I bet I could fit all the things I don't know inside of
the auto plant where you work

You told me you were working overtime that
December
Leaving my house at 1:30 in the morning
Four days a week, 30 days after we married

For all I know there was never any OT
For all ~~I know~~ suspect you were going to a doublewide
in Romeo at 1:30 every morning
Four hours before work

I bet I could fit everything I don't know inside of a
doublewide in Romeo, Michigan.

ALEXANDER

I know you will ask
So I'll go ahead and tell you
Since you always want to know
What I'm thinking about
When I masturbate

This morning I thought abt how I couldn't
Remember Nico's middle name
While I came two times
In the upstairs bed
Without you

I kept picturing the photo of his driver's license
He texted me
to prove we had the same bday
One night, mid pandemic
Feb, 2020

I probably didn't masturbate that night
I probably didn't think of anything that night either

I was always too shit-faced when talking to Nico
To think or masturbate (one of those is a lie; guess
which one) either.

Anyway, I don't want to know what you think abt,
sweetheart
So don't tell me
Alright? Ok?

Stupid shit men say

When nico said he wished he was half as good as me
What he meant was he wished he was in love w me
too

I bet kim Kardashian has someone to wax her
So she never has to know how much grey is in her
pubes now

MOUTH

You pulled a cigarette from the pack
W your mouth
like always

It still moved something in me
The part between my legs
Every time

An hour earlier you'd told me I was fucked up
"youre fucked up" you'd said "you're fucked up in the
head"

It was the way you always countered any argument I
offered
I couldn't argue you
I couldn't argue w logic like that
Anyhow

I am fucked up
I am fucked up in the head

And you
You pull cigarettes from the pack
With your mouth

And it moves something w/in me
Every fucking time.
It moves something within my fucked up head too

Idk what it is
Such a simple gesture
A lost art form

On my front porch in the wind
Me and your mouth
And my fucked up head

VEGAS

We were in vegas
But we were in the airport
This was a problem

"How do you get outside?" you asked
It'd been over six hours since you'd had a cigarette
Normally you smoked a pack and a half in six hours
That's thirty cigarettes

"I don't know" I said
"you have to get your bag in baggage, first, I guess"

I was dumb like that
We got to baggage and you walked outside
Left me standing alone in the southwest baggage area
Even though we'd flown delta

After a while you came back in
I wondered how many cigarettes you'd smoke;
I guess three, four, two, five.

We got in a fight in southwest baggage
Because neither of us knew how to find delta
And because you'd left me alone again to smoke a
cigarette outside

I didn't like being left alone anymore
I wanted a cigarette too but I was a sheep
I let rules and regulations and social norms control
me
Even though before I met you I thought I was the
rebel

Then I met you and I knew I wasn't shit

"I'm sorry," you said
Once we were outside, your luggage leaning on the
wall

You leaning between my thighs
"I love you so much," you said

I knew you loved me
But you loved something else more

That's okay
We all have to die someway
Someday

I wanted something I loved more too
But I didn't care too much about smoking or drinking
Or anything really

I didn't care enough about anything to break social
norms
To flub my nose at social rules

I just wrote stupid poems
And thought I was a rebel

I wasn't shit

I had to meet you to find this out

To make it up to me you paid too much for a car
To drive us to our hotel
You held my hand the hwole way
In the back of the overpriced car

"anywhere you want to stop? champagne? Liquor?
Cigarettes?"

A stop came w the service
You'd overpaid for
But you just wanted to get to the hotel
Get me in bed and fuck me

VEGAS II

It was the day before we were to marry
You wanted to dance
But Michigan state was playing Michigan
On the TV in the living room
Section of our hotel room

I told you id dance later
After the game

You got in bed to pout
Or you got in bed to nod out

I wasn't paying much attention

Michigan state was beating Michigan
I had had you put a small bet on the game

I was going to win $60

And tomorrow we would be married

I didn't pay attention to whether you were in bed
pouting
Or nodding out then

I should have paid more attention, I guess
But Michigan state was beating Michigan
And tomorrow we would be married
In a chapel w Elvis.

LET IT SNOW (aka: one month anniversary poem)

It's 6:08 (in the morning)
You've been gone almost an hour
I was awake in bed when you left (but you didn't know this)
I was sitting cross legged on the upstairs couch when you came back in for something
(a hat? a coat? Boots? I don't know what, I couldn't see)
I saw your face (my husband's face) for a second as you opened the door to leave (me) again

I don't know why I didn't call out (to you)
Or run down the stairs into your arms
I watched instead from the window like a child
As you cleaned your car of snow in our drive to leave (me)

At four in the morning I had sat outside on the porch w/out you
Smoking a cigarette, staring at the tree limbs so white, glistening
W new fallen snow that should have been romantic
Because I couldn't sleep
Wondering if it'd been snow instead of sleet earlier
If all this would have turned out differently

I could have gotten in bed beside you then (at 4)
I could have run outside to you while you cleaned your car (at 5)

I didn't know for sure I would cry
til you were backing out the drive

A radio station is playing "Let It Snow" currently, fyi -
I never knew a Xmas song could sound so cruel.

1970's Cinema

Baby

Let's go to the river park like we did before we got
married
Let's get donuts and burgers and eat them in the car
or
by the river
or
in bed
(anywhere
w you!)

(remember the woman on the bicycle, honey? The
one who yelled out: "Y'all are precious!" as we sat
curled around one another on the rock in the river
the day after the night you came to me a final time?)

Let's watch the horsey show in bed with champagne
And make out every ten minutes

Let's fuck and fuck and smoke in bed

Who ever said you can't smoke cigarettes in bed
anymore anyway?
I'm tired of envying old movie actors in 1970s cinema
– Cher, Kurt Russell, John Travolta

Who ever said we can't eat Taco Bell in bed, baby?
Who ever said

Neglect the Whole World Rather Than Each Other

I made the photograph of you pulling our Xmas tree
my computer screen background, honey
After you went to bed without me

Was it only a week ago you played Rod Stewart for
me on our front porch
And pulled me to you to dance in the cold?

I guess maybe it was two weeks ago, now

I still can't believe you had never heard that song

Anyway, I thought that was the height of romance:

My husband playing my favorite song on his smart
phone
And holding me to him on our porch
because he knows I never got asked to prom

I guess I have resigned myself not to sleep til you
come home
Even tho I slept a grand total of one hour and forty-
five mins last night
(11 - 12:45)

I hope you don't make me wait 48 hours

How long does the first real marital fight last?
I have to remember to ask Scott and Julia

I have to remember to ask you to play Rod Stewart
again
And to dance on our porch
Whenever you come back home, honey

Anyway, of course you went to prom
Anyway, I'm wearing a gold dress for you while I wait
even tho it's neither of our proms

Charlotte's Rules for a Happy Marriage

Why did you ask about New Year's, baby?
And why couldn't you remember being with me last
New year's Eve?

It terrifies me to think of what you can't remember

It terrifies me to think of you at Jazz's house
Surrounded by Jazz's dogs
Surrounded by others ...
like the set of a P T Anderson movie

Your days unfolding like the Catherine Deneuve's in
Belle de Jour

All because I don't know how to do drugs properly
Or own a pair of roller skates anymore

In my mind my face is already wet with the tears I
will cry
After your lover shoots me

It's true, I prayed you wouldn't be at the house when
I got back last night
But it's also true I prayed you would get in bed with
me
If you woke in the night or morning or whenever

It's ok to think I'm a bitch sometimes, honey
I'll steal your Adderall yet, baby

I don't know why I haven't stolen it yet!
If I was a real writer
Like Elizabeth Wurtzel
I would have snorted up all your Adderall weeks ago,
baby
But no one ever accused me of being a real writer
No one thinks your wife is a real writer at all, honey

Your Son's School Pic Is On My Fridge, Now Kiss Me

It was after you left
I noticed your son's school picture on my fridge

I always said it would be so much harder if he and I
had bonded
And now he and I are bonding and this is so hard

The difference is
The night I went for a walk in the snow
I came back and sat on the couch beside you
I didn't go straight to bed
I offered you a chance, baby

I may have been a bitch
But I was outside smoking w you

I may have been a bitch
But I let you drag me to bed
Like a good wifey

that's the difference, baby
this is so much harder
baby, why are you making this so hard?

Let's read Hemingway and make ice cream sundaes
Let's make love and make fun of writers on the
internet together!

Happy one month anniversary, baby
Please, come home.

Joan Didion is dead, 12/27 (a poem)

She should have killed herself a long long time ago
 like Hunter.
W a gun. in a corvette. Before her husband died.
The American dream.
anywy. Whtever.
She's dead.

I walk into fires willingly because I am a writer
I don't concern myself w burns – burns are words on
a page
Haha what a cheesy ass line to write!

You're right, baby, you chose the wrong woman

I will never be happy/satisfied w the TV/pills/
paycheck combo
I'm sorry I really don't like pizza either to tell you the
truth
It's ok tho
I'll still see you on some future lunch hour;
an hourly rated motel near the Ford plant

I won't be the one filing
I'm fine w being married and never seeing you
Like those odd cpls you hear other ppl talk abt

So mysterious!
(me, I mean; *I* will be *mysterious*, when I tell ppl this,
that I have a husband I haven't seen in x months, x
years, x decades)

how many years did joan live
w/out a husband

I can easily live that many w/out you, dear;
More

A man is only something to have

When you have nothing else

I don't so much mind being kicked out on Xmas day,
honey
I just minded that you didn't get me one book

That's how I could tell you were losing interest
For my bday you gave me at least three books, that I
Can remember; maybe four

Tennessee, Sylvia, a biography of the Bouveir sisters,
what else?

Joan didion is dead and I never even had a chance to
tell you abt her
I know if I ever kill myself in a car it should be a Ford,
not a Chevy, tho
On account of you

Remember when you thought I fucked the Bumble
guy
Cuz of the tampon wrapper in the toilet last week?

I told you baby
My pussy is always *so wet*

"Not a domestic vehicle in this parking lot" is
something I'll never forget
you saying after dinner on Easter

It's interesting the things we humans learn abt each
other
Human behavior, et al

Joan Didion eating eggs in a Corvette on the highway
Or her character anyway

Elizabeth Ellen inserting a slender tampon because
her pussy is so wet
Or her character anyway

(*slight bleeding after intercourse is normal* is all you could think abt when you saw the OB wrapper floating in the toilet after work last Tuesday)

my first marriage was ruined by a man's insecurities too; watchaknowabtthat

the irony – or at least, I believe this, unlike the examples in the Alanis Morrisette song, is an example of irony – here is that I was the one who got cheated on

what a perfect American dream

(incidentally, Joan Didion said infidelity was nothing to worry abt; haha JOAN!)

The truth is I fear equally: you coming back, you never returning

for the next two weeks
I will communicate solely with IG likes and posts

Joan Didion said infidelity is nothing to concern oneself with
But Joan Didion is dead
And I'm alive.

Anywy, I stole your favorite camo hat

I never even had time to go to social security and change my name

The only thing that concerns me now: who is going to help me get this ginormous
Christmas tree out of my house?

Joan Didion is dead and not a domestic vehicle in the parking lot.

Short xmas tree poem here

arbor day
my cooking

Dutiful

For [daughter's name]

How do I tell you that three/four hours after we left you,
Christmas night

My husband screamed at me
Called me a *fucking bitch*
In front of his seven year old son
Told me to *get the fuck out* of ~~the~~ his house

How do I tell you that?
How can anybody be so cruel?

How do I tell you I think I saw *her* idling in her truck
Two drives down, waiting on me to leave
While I packed my car, while I loaded the dog
That maybe he'd already texted her to come over
That they prob left that house together, the three of them -
A family, in tact, on Christmas
Drove together back to ~~her~~ their doublewide

While I drove home on a Michigan freeway
At one in the morning w my dog, and a ring I paid for myself
on my finger

I don't know how many days and nights will have to pass
Before I can utter any of the above words to you

I'm sorry

How do I tell you he was punishing me
For doing yoga and reading a novel (Play It As It Lays) on my laptop
In "my office" (read: *her* old room), instead of sitting

with him on the couch
Like a dutiful wife

Idk why *I'm not* cant be dutiful
Why I'm incapable of duty
Why I'm *insistently* consistently indutious

How do I tell you there are infinite ways
For a female heart to break/be broken

And only one of them is self-injurious
And only one is self-loathing

I'm sorry
I didn't want you ever to have to know any of this

Last poem for – (February 13, 2021)

AKA the three doors down

For two years I had a letter written to my daughter
On the big old Mac computer in my office/writing
room

The letter was in case of my death
Her first boyfriend's mom had died
And two years later, her second boyfriend's mom
Had died also

I am now older than the first boyfriend's mom
Slightly younger than the second boyfriend's mom
When each of them died

The letter was mostly to my daughter but there was
A part in there for you too
In the part for you I asked my daughter –
In the event of my death –
To send you a document I had titled "
Which was really a journal I had been writing since
we met
And hidden in a folder titled "
Begun as a way of voicing and (attempting to) deal w
my feelings
For you

I gave her your email address (in the letter)
So she could send you the document
In the event of my death

[Last sad/happy poem – a continuation of last poem]

Tomorrow is another valentine's day
I just realized
Yesterday I listened to you and --- on a podcast
Talking about your love story

It was interesting how 'your love story' and ours
Overlapped but there was no mention of me

It was as though I'd never existed
In your life

Which I guess is the feeling many women have –
Of erasure –
When they seek revenge or a man's comeuppance,
Whatever

When they publicly accuse
Or publicly victimize themselves

Publicly publicly publicly

I just want to make clear
When I said I would never publish these poems
It was under the belief we would always be friends
'permanent' you'd said, w regard to it
Our friendship, I mean

I deleted the old letter to my daughter
And wrote her a new one
In the event of my death

There is now no mention of you

It's hard to say if you'd have any interest in the journal
I kept
The two plus years we were *friends*...
Maybe the narcissist in you (matching the narcissist
in me, the narcissist in her)
Would

Smh

Anyway, I just realized tomorrow is another
valentine's day
The third since we met

I still love you
I wish you no ill will

I think we both found the person
We feel most ourselves with

So this isn't a sad poem (at all)
But a happy one

For the record, tho, I once made you a mix tape
And on it was the three doors down

Happy valentine's day

Postscript for –

At some point I thought maybe I was dying
Not in an emotional, love sick way
But in a literal physical one
While putting together the poems
In this collection this morning

And I thought, how appropriate would it be,
If I died assembling these love poems for -?

It almost makes me a little sad
I'm still breathing
I'm *not dead yet*
(like you famously said)
(like you not-famously once told me)

ALSO OUT ON FAR WEST

farwestpress.com

+1 (541) FAR-WEST